STILL HERE, STILL NOW

BOOKS BY ROBERT PACK

POETRY
Composing Voices
Elk in Winter
Rounding It Out
Minding the Sun
Fathering the Map: New and Selected Later Poems
Before it Vanishes: A Packet for Professor Pagels
Clayfeld Rejoices, Clayfeld Laments: A Sequence of Poems
Faces in a Single Tree: A Cycle of Dramatic Monologues
Waking to My Name: New and Selected Poems
Keeping Watch
Nothing but Light
Home from the Cemetery
Selected Poems (England)
Guarded by Women
A Stranger's Privilege
The Irony of Joy

POETRY FOR CHILDREN
The Forgotten Secret
Then What Did You Do?
How to Catch a Crocodile
The Octopus Who Wanted to Juggle

LITERARY CRITICISM
*Willing to Choose: Volition and Storytelling in Shakespeare's
    Major Plays*
Belief and Uncertainty in the Poetry of Robert Frost
The Long View: Essays on the Discipline and Hope of Poetic Form
Affirming Limits: Essays on Morality, Choice, and Poetic Form
Wallace Stevens: An Approach to His Poetry and Thought

Still Here, Still Now

ROBERT PACK

The University of Chicago Press / Chicago and London

Robert Pack is the Abernethy Professor of
Literature and Creative Writing Emeritus at
Middlebury College. He is the author of nineteen
books of poems, most recently *Rounding It Out* and
Elk in Winter, both published by the University of
Chicago Press.

The University of Chicago Press, Chicago 60637
The University of Chicago Press, Ltd., London
© 2008 by The University of Chicago
All rights reserved. Published 2008
Printed in the United States of America
17 16 15 14 13 12 11 10 09 08   1 2 3 4 5
ISBN-13: 978-0-226-64415-8 (cloth)
ISBN-10: 0-226-64415-4 (cloth)

Library of Congress Cataloging-in-Publication Data
Pack, Robert, 1929–
    Still here, still now / Robert Pack.
        p. cm.
    ISBN-13: 978-0-226-64415-8 (alk. paper)
    ISBN-10: 0-226-64415-4 (alk. paper)
    I. Title.
    PS3566.A28S75 2008
    811'.54—dc22

                                2007039509

♾ The paper used in this publication meets the
minimum requirements of the American National
Standard for Information Sciences—Permanence
of Paper for Printed Library Materials, ANSI Z39.48-
1992.

For Patty all the way

. . . and laugh

At gilded butterflies . . .

—WILLIAM SHAKESPEARE (*King Lear*, V, 3)

CONTENTS

ACKNOWLEDGMENTS

Grateful acknowledgment is made to the editors of the following publications in which some of the poems in this book first appeared:

Academic Questions: "Pride and Laughter"

"Flute Music at Noon," "Happiness," and "Tamaracks" are reproduced from *Prairie Schooner*, volume 81, issue 2 by permission of the University of Nebraska Press. Copyright © 2007 by the University of Nebraska Press.

"Mountain Meditation" first appeared in the anthology *Poems Across the Big Sky*, edited by Lowell Jaeger. Cincinnati: Many Voices Press, 2007.

I. FOR YOU AND YOU

ANOTHER MARCH

Another March, and in chilled trees thick sap
Begins to surge — a fact so fundamental I
Embrace its deep impersonality;
Yet it is I who feel it even though
I surely could be anyone. So, too,
Our life together, reaching back
A half a century, recaptures you
While planting daffodils in autumn mist,
Gleaming tomato stalks in May, as if
I read about us in a gilded book:
Our story's rounded with its end, just as
Returning seasons change and merge —
The thrum of summer I remember as
A hummingbird suspended at a rose —
Becoming one, as we are one, and full
With ripeness and with ruddy ripening,
Forever vanishing, forever there,
Forever gone and irreplaceable.

FACING YOU

When I say, circle, I select the moon
Or sun, or I select my wedding band;
I offer to expanding space this plucked
Revolving apple in my outstretched hand.

And for variety, elliptical
Eggplant or tapered pear also can please,
The streaked breast of a bleating meadowlark,
The reaching arc of flowing willow trees.

Look there, my love, an indescribable
Meandering of yellow butterflies
Descends upon an oval pond crowded
With luminescent lily pads — like eyes

That contemplate swirled clouds as if
Even elusiveness might be defined,
The vanished years we share, dissolved
Into a garden's purple mist: a kind

Of tendered thankfulness. And so I name
Your spirit's likeness with fresh forms without,
For turning inward to myself alone
There's only fading thought to think about.

PAUL SEES MORE LIGHT

I fainted dead away beside the plate
Of juicy shrimp that rainy evening meant
To gather critics there to celebrate
My lecture on poetic form, intent.

Revived among dark faces circling me —
There was my literary ally, Paul,
Who leaned down hazy close — I could well see
Distress upon his sunken face for all

The losses our long friendship shared; concern
From him passed into me and made me limp.
A doctor took my leaping pulse to learn,
Was I allergic to such foods as shrimp?

Up from unconscious depths came my reply:
"No, but I am allergic to free verse."
The "Oh" that lunged from Paul's tight lips, his sigh
On hearing my smart-ass remark (no worse,

I think, than some he'd heard before) remains
The most melodious to sooth me when
My stressed-out heart speaks of its beating pains,
Its bare regrets. Paul told the doctor then:

"He's not yet ready to give up the fight;
I'll know when Bob's near death; he'll be all right."

FLUTE MUSIC AT NOON

I watch you walking with your flute
Head high across a purple clover field;
The air is still, warm leaves are mute,
Silence is still to be revealed.

Flute notes upon moist lips just mean
Just what they are, a silver melody,
Expressing nothing in the scene.
No correspondence I can see

Between your aura and the hue
Of purple sweetness swirling in the breeze
Is needed to enhance the true
Attraction that the aching bees

Perceive, as I perceive the notes
Composed together, one by silver one,
On which your passing presence floats
Until you vanish in the sun.

YOU ARE THE ONE

Here's what we know — incredible
as it may seem, since we can't get
our minds around the concept of
blank nothingness: Space/time began
when Big Bang generated everything;
that's right, there was no time, no anything,
before the Big Bang start, and so the laws
that govern nature as we know them now —
the interplay of energy and mass,
the formula E equals m c squared —
came into being when space/time commenced.
    But whoa! How did those laws know what
to formulate if they were not
already written somehow in the void,
in some Platonic realm, even before
there was a single universe in which
the laws of math could operate — perhaps
as paradigms for freedom within fate,
or maybe for the need to hold desire
within some limits of constraint?
    Did not these laws then have to be,
from sheer necessity, transcendent laws —
laws that a math professor might
be tempted to define, "Pi in the sky,"
laws that the wild-browed Einstein speculated
God Himself would have to follow since
He'd have no choice if He desired
to fabricate one universe that worked?

How can these two conditions equally
be true at once? I'm sure you'd like to know.
How can the cosmic laws of physics come
into Big Bang existence only when
existence starts its evolutionary journey
to its consummation in inventing love,
and yet precede existence in some realm
where numbers dwell, timeless and absolute,
where Pi unfolds into an unknown end?
My mind whirls in a vertigo when I
attempt to comprehend such things.

　　　　　But that's enough of small talk for tonight;
all that I meant to say is that you are
the only one, the one and only one
to hold me steady in this swirl of stars
and dust in an expanding universe.
What chance is there you'll go to bed with me?

THE BLUE VASE

After our son was born
(he's now gone out into the world)
my wife acquired a blue transparent vase
that she discovered among junk
congested at an antique store;
she placed it on a table
by our kitchen window
where it would reflect
eastern then southern light
of the reliably revolving sun.
Over the years, I've passed it by
a thousand times or more,
admiring its glimmering blue
though only at a fleeting glance.
Yesterday as white sun arose,
the blue vase seemed to beckon me,
compelling me to pause
exactly in the interval
through which I was about to pass.
Transfixed, spellbound, I stood
there in the morning's ambient glow
an hour or more, watching
the sun's first beams caress
the curving surface of the vase,
casting a star of stippled light
upon the table top of inlaid ivory
as if a message or a sign
had been encoded there.

Still in a kind of trance, I wondered: What
could this reflected light
in interplay with its reflection on
a tabletop — on which my wife
had set a basket of bananas, oranges,
green apples, purple grapes and plums —
what could this cornucopia of color
be symbolic of? And what had that design,
contrived by law and chance,
to do with our son's birth
or with my wife's fortuitous
selection of a lucent vase
to apprehend the morning light?
Surely, I thought, some purpose
must be there to be discerned
to complement that radiating harmony
of ripened fruit and colored light.
And then it came to me as in
a counter-revelation:
I'd tried in vain to find
some revelation there beyond
what she had carefully arranged
and that precisely was the failure I
could now possess and call my own.
All that I needed to believe was true
had been composed only
with blue light and with varied fruit,
only with multicolored fruit
and blue reflected light
reflecting into deeper blue.

MOUNTAIN DAWN

From where I watch in my pine-paneled room,
the mountain range, about ten miles away
and to the east, displays its silhouette
as it obscures the rising sun; and then,
just as the sun appears, an edge of light
ignites the snow-packed mountain top and brings
its crevices and slopes into relief.
   And so a day in the home stretch begins,
although my thoughts turn to beginnings
other than my own: Big Bang, of course, comes first
when, out of sheer nothingness space and time
commence with just a quantum fluctuation
according to fixed laws we still obey;
this idea — absence, nothing, nothingness —
I try to grasp in feeling as in thought.
   And then the leap miraculous to life,
stupendous trick of prestidigitatious
replication by a genius molecule
with consequences unforeseeable
even beyond divine imagining
is what in reverence I dwell upon.
   But so, too, death was born, and that would not
have been so bad if consciousness of death,
what most we have become, and are,
had not inflicted us to live with loss
made permanent, aching the more
the more we love. Only the animals
were spared, only the teeming grasses and

the sweet serenity of swaying trees.
The birth of inwardness made us suppose
that we must be some awful aberration,
some grave mistake nature had stumbled on.
   Mother oh mother, the beginning of
your irreversible oblivion
began a year ago; I picture your wide eyes
and your round face with an astonished look,
asking what could have separated us
after a lifetime of our talking every
indistinguishable day — talking of what?
What does it matter now? It seemed as if
words were enough to keep us in our lives,
to keep blank, gaping nothingness away,
back in its quantum void where absence is
not burdened with awareness of itself,
or where the sunrise on a mountain peak
illuminates only azure sky, only
the shadowed slopes and shaded crevices.

NO RECONCILING

No touch remains but shivering;
Wan autumn's misty warmth is spent;
No reconciling, no forgiving
The way you were, the way you went.

Hunched crows sit silent on a branch
Where raucous cries rent the stunned air;
I see white emptiness advance;
I see your absence everywhere.

I see you where a butterfly
Once rested on a sunstruck stone
Blindly ablaze as you walked by
Alone — content to be alone.

I see you where the dwindling stream
Fumbles and arcs around the bend;
I know such disappearance means
Endings recalled prolong the end —

As I do here in my embracing
Shifting apparitions of loose shade,
Defining what I now am facing:
The flutterings your last light made.

TORNADO CONSOLATION

One cannot tell a hospital stood here;
The rubble just as well could be a church.
How many are still buried? We all fear
More dead will turn up in tomorrow's search.

No water, but a coke machine still works.
A radio without a listener
Plays songs of unrequited love; the quirks
And twists of human longing rend the air.

There is no one to blame, no one to hate,
And yet the dead remain exactly so;
Profoundly mute, they've nothing to relate,
Though I imagine they'd be cheered to know

This was not caused by terrorists within
Our midst, or punishment for human sin.

MOONLIGHT MIRRORINGS

I woke from midnight sleep to watch
The full moon shimmer in the lake;
Moon doubling mirrored in my mind,
Reminding me for her lost sake

That's what thought does — thought multiplies
Upon remembered thought to cling
To what is gone and make it stay
In glimmers of past vanishing.

But she stays gone except perhaps
For my uncertain saying so,
And so reflections of the moon,
The way the wash of waters go,

Reveal how once I waited there
Beside the lake, expecting her
To step out from behind a tree
And make what thought desired occur.

And there I am, still there beside
Moon water sipping at the shore,
As her not coming comes again,
Repeating what I never saw.

THE STORY'S END

I'd like to live on for a while —
a day, a year, a century —
not merely for the sake
of hanging on, but to find out
if humankind is able to avoid
nuclear war, the final war
of clashing ideologies.
          In this survivor's interval
I could continue to enjoy
the pleasures that allow me
to forget all goals beyond
just ordinary satisfactions like
my strolling by a lake
with purple sunset in the clouds
and swallows swooping from their nests,
making smooth arcs
that seem to organize the hills.
          And yet my deepest motive
to extend my life — despite
the evening sun's consoling warmth,
despite the wind's low melody
among the wafted willow leaves —
is to discover how
the human story ends, and thus
to know what I might make
my one life mean right now.
          I circle slowly round the lake,
walking in rhythm with myself;

I sway a little with the swaying lily pads,
returning to the house we built
so many unrecorded pleasures past
where now you wait for me
beneath the doorway's shaded arch.
      Why can't my homecoming
suffice? Why can't I be content
just with a greeting, an embrace,
the image of two swallows
as they swoop and dip and spin?
What greedy curiosity demands
I know if humankind survives
until the sun collapses on itself —
an ending I can comprehend.
      I see you standing there
within the doorway's gathered shade,
wafted by music from the willow tree,
thinking the thought I can't avoid,
thinking my questioning is vain.
Shall I construe my wish to know
if everything we love gets lost
as an attempted hymn of praise?
Or must I chant it as an elegy?

LOGICAL SPECULATION

For sure, it's easier to fabricate
A virtual universe, a fake,
Than one that's actual, composed of stuff
Obeying laws that make life possible,
Including consciousness, if given fourteen
Billion years, but under fixed conditions
So particular and finely tuned, like getting heads
Four-hundred coin flips in a row, that they
Defy chance as a workable hypothesis.
The odds against our really being here
Strain all credulity, so maybe it's
Not that far-fetched to speculate a man —
Let's say a brilliant scientist who was
Rejected by a woman whom he loved —
Light years away in a dim galaxy,
Decided to design on his computer
His own version of a world that is
Inhabited by people who believe
That they are absolutely real, and that
Their species' history of violence
Actually occurred. They take on faith
The fabrication of a warring past
Within the fabrication they're alive
Right now, bearing the brunt of present time.
Dramatic and compelling, yes,
And yet these people realize their life
Seems flawed, imperfectly contrived, as I
Myself confess to that suspicion since

There's something quite incredible about
What surely is excessive suffering —
As if our world's designing scientist
Had been compelled to share his emptiness,
As if he might be someone else's thought.
How's that scenario for likelihood?

Tell me, could a computer genius with
His heart's desires remaining unresolved,
No matter how advanced the culture he
Inhabited, let his own suffering
Affect him when inventing somebody
As kind as you, although he knows you are
A simulation? And, a simulation, too,
I walk along a tangled woodland path
In flaming autumn, missing you, your touch,
Your undulating voice, baffled because
Your absence is so palpable to me.

And so I picture you strolling the beach,
Circled by raucous gulls, where you once lived
Before your mother died, recalling how
You greeted me that windy afternoon
While standing in the doorway of your house,
Inviting me to step into the shade
Of inner rooms, their purple atmosphere,
Seem so unreal as I remember them.

But they seem real as well, the colors and
The silken shade, and even unreality,
My thinking about thinking about thought,
Seems real, although I cannot hold your image
Steady in my mind. I ache for you —
Perhaps the same ache that he aches —
Your presence and your whisper and your touch,

Wishing to bring you back and hold you here,
Before the wind I feel within my bones
Blows your remembered face away like sand,
Leaving gray driftwood lifting up gaunt arms,
Before his bright computer screen fades out to black.

GRANDSON

His father piled the colored blocks
up to the level of his eyes, so he,
a force of Nature like a blast of wind,
could knock them down,
knowing his father right on clue
would build the tower up again
for him to scatter on the rug, as if
it represented the whole universe,
and yet without harm done. The blocks
seemed tumbled in perpetuity —
the future right before my eyes
to contemplate, for me,
the father of a father of a son.
And he would turn his head
to make sure that I was observing him,
so that his laughter spanned
our generations there, spreading from him
to his observing father, then to me,
the father of a father of a son,
and back again, renewed, revitalized,
and ready to again move on.
I was astounded he assumed
that he was living in a funny world —
a sense he did not learn from me
or even from his dad; no doubt
he had been born possessing it —

a gift that Nature in its laws
of continuity bestowed on him.

    And so, when perched upon
his high-chair throne, discarding food
this way and that as if there never
could be famine in the world,
feasting with the entire family,
his mom, his grandmother, his aunt,
the would-be chieftain of the clan
clapped his commanding hands
and beat them on the tray — applause
for me to imitate, and him to imitate
my imitation. This, too, appeared to him
hilarious, and every one of us
joined the hilarity; laughter, for sure,
had power to suffuse the universe.

    But after mom had put him into bed,
and sleep suspended laughter in the night,
his father told me of the operation
that he faced, his shoulder muscles
had to be tied up to hold the bones
within their sockets, and that meant
he'd have to change his occupation
as a landscaper; he'd have to start again
defining who at heart he was,
no longer keeper of the shrubs and trees,
stripped down to his identity
as husband and as father to a son.

    What laughter then could I
recover from such stunning news?
There was indeed a message

to be heeded from these facts: we all
must persevere no matter what
the obstacles; our love of children
must remain enough to keep us
doing what we have to do.
But is there laughter to be found
In grim necessity, in Nature howling out
what seems to us the logic of a whim?

      And thereby I proclaimed this to be so;
apostle of absurd defiance, I
crashed my fist down upon the wooden table
where we sat, and then my son,
in instantaneous response,
slammed his hand down so hard
he made the flaming candles
shudder in their wicks. We caught
the glitter in each other's eyes,
and in that moment we both realized
a revelation had occurred — a revelation
that released our laughter once again.

      We laughed beyond all reason
and beyond restraint, our uproar like
a banquet of the drunken gods,
our mad tears overwhelming us,
until our mutual cacophony
awoke the baby from protecting sleep
with cries confused and terrified.

      Confused myself, hopeful without
convincing evidence, I still
have one remaining blessing to bestow:
the wish that some unbidden day my grandson

will inherit laughter of another kind —
laughter most human in its sympathy —
to add to what already lies within
his muscles and his bones, when he,
whose voice contains wild mountain winds,
becomes his generation's caretaker,
the father of a father of a son.

COMFORTING

I am aware you are aware
I think about what it might well be like
to live your life, to wake each day
into a body made of hidden places
different from my own,
to share our sorrows and our fears,
and thereby to be comforted.

As evening thickens in the room,
encroaching on the changing shapes
and colors of the dwindling fire,
I feel your fingers reach out
to my cheeks to touch, to soothe,
like incandescent words that know
precisely what they mean to mean.

And so I feel that you must feel
precisely what I feel
in feeling that I know
what your most hidden feelings are,
touching my cheek, touching my thoughts,
as words — like reaching fingers — touch
when rightly used and thus believed,
thus rightly felt and understood.

And so I know you know
what soothes my mind even
as deepened evening light
obscures our tightened room,
evoking in us the same sense
of darkness and of loss — of binding loss

that holds the two of us together
in what feels like an embrace
as I throw wood upon the fire
as if it's not too late to light
some long-extinguished star.
      Your fingers on my face pull back,
their cooling sense remaining
even though their touch
has been relinquished to the dark;
the fire flares from inside itself,
the yellow orange and the orange red
linger a second in their afterlight,
and yet the room still closes in:
I know that you can tell
I now must be envisioning
some great collapse of space and time,
some final black-hole pull,
consuming everything that we
have clung to, everything we've loved.
      The dwindling flames recede,
as all flames do and must,
the orange yellow and the orange red,
dissolve into one dense,
undifferentiated dark — a dark I know
you know I know you know
that seems to be expecting our return
into some unimaginable realm,
deeper than knowing what each other knows,
beyond our need for comforting.

II. SHORT AND TALL TALES

REINCARNATION

I told my friend that in my former life
I'd been a mother duck; "Impossible,"
Was his immediate reply, "you can't
Repeat yourself in two lives in a row."
But I contend he's wrong, for when I was
Sixteen I had two luminous white ducks
And kept them in a pen I tended with
Devoted care. The hen laid six sleek eggs,
And every morning at the surge of dawn
I checked her nest to see if all was well.
     One night, as the indifferent stars looked on,
A weasel stole into their hutch and ate the eggs
That I alone had been assigned to guard —
Though one spared egg was only cracked, and when,
Amid ripped feathers scattered all around,
I tapped it with my middle fingernail,
A baby duck popped out. I'm sure you've heard
Of imprinting; well then, I was the one,
The moving thing, chosen to be the first
That duckling saw; and so it was, Nature
Herself had thus decreed I was assigned
To be that duckling's Mom. So picture him
Following close behind me where I walked
Along the fern-dense path or by the pond
Or back into his hutch when bedtime came.
I'd put him in the pocket of my shirt,
His head poked out, when I sat down to read;
I swear he was especially content

If I would read to him out loud — which shows
How much of human meaning, too, resides
In intonation and one's tone of voice.
Men would be wise to take account of this.

      Nothing concerned me but the welfare of
That baby duck, and it delighted me
To learn, many confused years later, that
Right after birth, for several months, embryos
Are female until a hormone-driven rush
Of grim testosterone turns some genes male.
And so it cannot be denied; I started out
With Mom potential which by chance I was
Permitted to fulfill, despite my friend's
Assertion of impossibility.

      At summer's end, I knew the time had come
To send my duck into the world, and so
I put him in the pond and said, "Goodbye,"
Wishing him happiness — what else can Moms
Or any parent do? He visited the pond
At intervals, when yellow maple leaves
Graced the still water mirroring the clouds,
Then he was gone, although I watched for him
Through many amber summers afterwards.

      I wonder now what my next phase will hold,
And if, when by the pond, I'll see my duck
And recognize him among other ducks
Amid a whir of whiteness as they rise,
Or if my friend is right to think that I
Have used up my identity as Mom
And better get on with a father's life,
Wary of weasels and swift violence.

LITERARY RAVENS

It was a sparkling Saturday in June —
A perfect day to drive an hour to town,
To browse the open marketplace,
Bump into chatty friends,
And purchase the fresh vegetables
Grown by our local farmers
And laid out in luminous display:
Lettuce and radishes, carrots,
Baby potatoes — white and red —
Scallions and spinach, testifying how
Amazing Mother Nature is
When She's in harmony
With cultivating human care.
Returning home, we found the floor
Of our garage completely strewn
With bottles, cans, discarded paper,
Orange and banana peels.
I realized that I'd neglected
To roll down the rumbling door,
Thus leaving garbage pails
Exposed to swooping ravens
Who had emptied them. And here's
Where my adoring hymn to Nature,
My domestic saga of contentment,
Touches on what some of you,
Only the skeptical, incredibly
May find incredible.

Corrected papers on the floor,
Included drafts of odes that I
Had recently composed about
These shining birds, praising
Their patience and persistence,
Their unusual intelligence,
Evoked their curiosity and, no doubt,
Their vanity, as well, and tempted them
To read my rhapsodizing poems,
Translating them into their own
Raucous vernacular.

They had, of course, admired them
And searched the teeming bounty
Of the tumbled garbage pails
For every luscious word
Their appetites could find therein.
I hope that you'll agree
No other explanation can account
For how the poems' revisions were
Deliberately arranged
Upon the telltale floor which otherwise
Would have to be explained merely
By chance or randomness.

And in that glow of revelation I,
Enraptured and serene, considered how
Poetic art conjoined with Nature
Make a pair, as man and woman do,
Helpmates and complements,
And how, when merged with mind,
With soaring, speculating mind,
Inchoate Nature can reach out

In order to express Herself,
Thus giving substance to the very thought
Expressed, adding to what is real,
Transforming ordinary fact
Into the highest visionary form.
          My moment of transcendence passed —
Such moments, we all know, can't be
Sustained — and then my job was just
To tidy up the aggravating mess,
Restoring order to its mundane state.
My wife called out when I was done,
"Next time we go to town, make sure the door
Is closed so ravens can't get in."
I felt chagrined, I felt let down —
I kicked the damn offending door —
But wishing to assure her that
One mess like this was quite enough
To help complete a perfect day,
All I could think to say was "Nevermore."

HAPPINESS

So what then might you single out
as the most happy moment of your life?

The memory that leaps first into mind
is swimming in a lake to nowhere
in particular, feeling my body's glide,
easy and smooth, stroke by untiring stroke,
as if I could go on forever with
no need to rest, no need even to think
of anything but being where I was,
right there, right then, the luminescent water
sliding out and dripping from the curve
made by my lifted arm, catching the sparks
of slanting red and orange evening light.

Is that all you might mean by happiness,
just bodily well being, the illusion
nothing will change — the moment so complete,
contained within itself, that it might seem
as if it were eternity? Shouldn't
your one defining moment be much more
than fleeting pleasure, more than freedom from
disturbing thoughts of time, ongoing flux?
Shouldn't high happiness involve someone
you love for whom you make a sacrifice
to carry you beyond your single self?

Well, we were driving home that foggy night,
having an argument, the crudest kind
of argument about how much she spent
on a dumb hat, and what made it still worse —
the hat was shiny black, a color she
well knew I hate; hot red or cobalt blue
would say to me that she had purchased it
to please my taste, fashion be damned,
but no, it was all black, prophetic black.
A car pulled out from the oncoming lane —
there was no way of my avoiding it,
so what I chose to do was spin our car
sharp to the right hoping the impact of
the crash would land on me and maybe she'd
survive. In that huge instant as the glass
splashed on my face like sudden water from
a swimmer's arm, before my widened mind
ironically went black, I was content
with what I'd done, more than content; I'm sure,
beyond my fear, I felt pure happiness,
the kind you asked about. I'd passed the test
that my philosophy required: I was
the person I'd prepared myself to be.

> Does that defining moment still provide
> meaning enough to take you to the end
> your dark philosophy foresees — and can
> proving you truly loved her, still outweigh
> all that you know about the suffering
> nature inflicts upon us all, to which we add
> the special curse of human cruelty:
> betrayal and ingratitude and bombs?

When I woke from the week-long coma I
was buried in, the busty nurse told me
that I kept blurting out, "the hat, the hat!"
and though she couldn't fathom what I'd meant,
she knew then that I'd make it back to health.
My wife, wearing her hat, arrived to fetch
me from the hospital, and I'll admit,
black as it was, the hat looked good on her.
I laughed and she laughed in response and I
laughed at her laughing, she in turn at mine,
and maybe I should rank that moment as
the ultimate in happiness I have enjoyed
because we shared absurd defiance without
hope that must rely upon a wish
for some transcendent meaning to emerge.

        That's evidence enough for you to claim
        your faith in laughter will enable you
        to make it to the end; that's why you find
        delectable the knowledge that before
        "pursuit of happiness" was linked with "life
        and liberty," by father Jefferson,
        "pursuit of property," Locke's pithy phrase,
        expressed a goal that's realizable.
        How lowdown practical, how crass, how crude,
        how undeluded and inspired Locke was!

I must confess I secretly had hoped
you would have held out longer in requiring
that I embrace something more than laughter,
more than blood sacrifice that can't escape
the blackness in its need to rescue loss

by one's embracing loss — something noble like
the world remade through visionary art.
That's it! I'll write a book called HAPPINESS,
certain to make me rich — people will pay
good money for advice on how to live.
I'll buy a farm with lots of acreage and build
a mansion for my wife. Some comic scenes
will be quite autobiographical.
And though dazed children starve in Africa
as mothers wail up to the skies for them,
and soldiers cut the throats of prisoners
as always they have done, what harm, I ask,
can the pursuit of carefree happiness
do to whatever pleasures that mere chance
or universal law indifferently
allow: a hat tipped toward the waiting void,
or swimming on a summer afternoon
to some shore nowhere in particular?

FOUR GUYS CROSS MONTANA

"The Last Best Place," UNOFFICIAL STATE MOTTO

The one alone remaining of us four,
yet stubbornly alive, with memory
enough to care, I still recall
our journey to Montana
just to see new sights — mountains
imposing in austere indifference,
moose or big-horned sheep or elk,
yet what I treasure most is how
we made each other laugh;
I still can hear triumphant laughter
rippling down the blur of years.
    We drove across the rolling prairie,
undulating like a female body's curves,
enjoying our own teasing company;
by midday, voices harsh with thirst,
we stopped for lunch and beer
in a small village indistinct
except for the big-breasted bartender
at the CELESTIAL BAR AND GRILL,
where right above the mirror facing us
a bold announcement there proclaimed:
IN GOD WE TRUST — THE REST OF YOU PAY CASH.
Defiantly we did.
    On our way out of town we made
a wrong turn on a one-way street,
guffawing all together since
the arrow on the pole had slipped
and now was pointing down, confirming

what we knew already of our fate,
proud fornicators that we were —
or wished to be. And then
more confirmation came
as the town prophet on the street corner,
sporting his jaunty cowboy hat,
deranged or drunk, warned us
the world was coming to an end.

      We took delight in speculating that
four ordinary guys obsessed with ass
had been elected to receive
personal revelation of apocalypse,
and this delectable idea
was further cause for our hilarity —
as if hilarity was born
within the marrow of our bones.

      "It's fun to share such fun!"
we freely, blissfully concurred,
and got back in our car to travel on,
deciding that we'd spend the night
at some extravagant resort
and stalk girls by the swimming pool,
sharing gross jokes whose innuendos
celebrated body parts as if
sleek limbs or loins or lips
were able to enjoy life mindlessly;
but then to elevate our thoughts
we chose to take a scenic route —
nature in her sublimity —
along a recommended mountain road.

      As we descended through the pass
of clustered evergreens, we witnessed

pale blue lupine in patched sunny intervals
and mule deer grazing by the road;
we were content as they, at peace, serene,
and I still hear triumphant laughter
rippling down the blur of years.
We passed a windless lake
reflecting the whole mountainside
and then, together, all at once, we saw
a painted sign with upturned mouth
and dotted eyes — a smiley face —
above a weathered cemetery gate,
which read: THIS IS THE LAST BEST PLACE.

THE STUTTERER

     The story that I promised you
about my friend, the stutterer —
well, here it is: We'd argue if
we ought to send our troops to war,
and when it looked as if I'd win
the argument, he'd blurt, "Easy, b-Bud,
for you to say," and I'd be stopped
by laughter not by reasoning.
     He told me he once had a friend
who stuttered worse than he. His friend
explained how it began: when he
was just a skinny brat at camp,
his bunkmate was a stutterer,
and he, with boyhood cruelty,
would mimic the embarrassed kid;
his joking made him stupidly
oblivious to that kid's pain.
By summer's end, the mimicker
became the stutterer; he has
remained afflicted to this day.
But that's not where my story ends.
     I have a student in my class
who stutters when he's called upon;
a gutsy kid, he does not let
this sole impediment prevent
him from expressing his ideas.
After he spoke in class last week,
to my appalled astonishment,

I stuttered when responding to
his stuttering, as if some monster
guilt had warped my empathy;
for the remaining hour of class,
I willed myself to slow down my
remarks so that my words came out
composed as I intended them.

       The fear that I could not control
the words that make me who I am,
according to my choice, disturbed
my breathing and my blood, and now
I'm almost stopped by this same fear
I'll stutter as I speak to you,
and you won't want to marry me.

ARGUING FRIENDS

Whether we fought because we disagreed
Or simply just enjoyed a good debate,
Was hard to tell, but politics, of course,
Brought forth the passions closest to our hearts,
With baseball next. We both were Yankee fans
From boyhood on, but I, disdaining all
The dough they had to spend, switched my allegiance to
The Sox, rejecting my past ties, gaining
An Evil Empire to do battle with.
We differed most in our opposing views
Of whether we were right to send our troops
Into Iraq, whether democracy was possible
In that part of the world or not. I thought
We had to try, but feared the worst: that war,
Atomic war — since human nature has
Not changed — would come about, and he feared most
That liberties at home would soon be lost.
We each respected what the other thought,
Yet hints of strain were inescapable.
What bliss when finally the Red Sox won
The series after being three games down;
Justice achieved its shining moment in
An otherwise uncaring universe
Where Yahweh left us to defend ourselves
Among a multitude of enemies —
A sentiment we shared. Sometimes
We'd fight about an issue less intense
Than war; he was an advocate of Choice:

A woman's body is entirely
Her own, and she should have the option when
To keep the fetus as she so desired.
　　　But still I think that I one-upped him with
My definition of parental choice,
Claiming that parents had a moral right
To opt for an abortion of their child—
Since they're the ones supporting him—until
The age of twenty-one or else until
The child is able to support himself,
Whichever happens to come earliest.
　　　So on it went, neither of us giving way,
Unable to persuade the other who
Had made the more compelling case, and yet
We both remained committed to the idea
Dialogue, debate, and reason were
The sole alternatives to force for nations
When their faiths or ideologies
Or economic interests clashed. If just
We two could not become a model for
How reconciliation might occur,
What then could worldly hope be based upon?
　　　Once he invited me to dine with him
At an expensive Chinese restaurant
In swank downtown New York. A six-course meal
Was followed, as required, by ritual,
With fortune cookies, and my pick proclaimed:
Confucius says: "A fool just by himself
Can't win a war." Surely, he'd written that
As some kind of a subtle joke, contrived
To re-enforce a point, but what it was
I only could surmise and had to guess.

His cookie read: "Confucius says a fool
Alone cannot negotiate a peace."
If he, as I suspected, had arranged
To write them both, how did he know which one
Would go to him and which one I'd select?
      He smiled and paid the whopping bill, then reached
Into his bulging pocket and pulled out
His Yankee cap and placed it jauntily
Upon his head; in reciprocity
I graciously doffed back to him my old
Red Sox chapeau. Then we walked out, my arm
Around his shoulder, his on mine, together
In the neon multicolored night,
The clear cacophony of the shrill street.

THE TEACHER SHAKES UP HIS CLASS

Most of the students in my Shakespeare class
Had come from homes with violated vows;
They doubted that their lives would safely pass
Without nuclear war or private woes:
Their failure to find meaning in the mess
Of all the battling ideologies,
Their fear that daily work was meaningless.
The bard's *Macbeth*, although a rousing read,
Did not depict for them the harmony
In marriage or in childrearing they sought.
I watched the students scrutinizing me.
"Have you been married long?" one blurted forth.
"Forty-five years" said I. Their breathless pause
Was followed by spontaneous applause.

BROTHERS

The month was February and the time
Just when the moon comes up and shadows stretch
Across the silver undulating snow.
It was bone-aching cold, and windy, too,
With swooshing noise that blundering wind makes
When bludgeoning among the evergreens —
So dark their outlines merged into a blur.
My wife and I were dozing by the fire
When rhythmic knocking at our carved oak door
Disturbed our separate reveries, although
Our sleepy conversation took us swooping back
To when our children lived at home, which seemed
A storyteller's once-upon-a-time ago.
We had assumed that no one at that hour
Would visit us, remote and solitary in the woods
Where we then lived, so I felt apprehension
When I opened up the door and saw a woman
In a cape which shuddered in the wind
Like wearied wings still pulsing after flight.
Her forehead caught the moonlight's silver glow
Obscuring her dark eyes, which made me feel
That she was watching me from far away
Or from some fading, legendary time.
I asked her in, but she remained unmoved
As wind gusts kept on flapping at her cape.
She claimed in her raised tones that she had come
To pass along an urgent message, yet
She wouldn't tell me what it was until

She knew for sure I was the one she sought,
And she insisted I reveal some things
That would disclose my true identity.
I told her that our children had left home,
But that we were determined to remain
Here in our hidden forest home, despite
Its isolation and slick icy storms,
Where I was working on a book about
How people must endure life-numbing loss —
Try to endure is what I meant to say
As swirling wind kept swishing at the door.
  "You have a brother," said the messenger,
"A twin your mother gave away at birth,
Thinking that she could not support two boys;
He has no children of his own and needs
A family's support before it is
Too late; he asks if he can contact you
Or if you feel that too much time has passed.
The fact is he's not well — a truth that you
Must take into account, although you
May be wondering about my motives
For suddenly arriving unannounced
On such a windy, frozen night as this.
My reason is I think you need each other,
And I've come because I want to help;
Does that seem unbelievable to you?"
  I was so shocked, so unprepared for news
Like this that no words came to me; a moan,
A little moan, foamed at my twitching lips
And bubbled there, but would not shape itself
As thought. What thought? What could I think?

Should I consider this good news or bad —
A brother reaching out to me for help?
My heart went out to him as if he were
Indeed my twin, and yet this surely was
A grave intrusion on my inner life.

    "He really is not well," the messenger
Went on as if in answer to the words
I failed to say; "perhaps that can explain
Why you two look alike, especially
When shadows sculpt the downturn of your mouths.
I think a rumor's reached him that you are
Completing a new book; you might assume
He'd like to be in it and that he wants
The life you have not shared with him to be
Recorded there. I think he thinks you can
Give substance to his ache of emptiness."

    "What kind of airy substance could that be?"
I queried her, assuming that she knew,
As if she had once lived and cared for him,
As if his sorrows were her sorrows too.
"I'll have to make him up," I said, "invent
A life out of what might have been; maybe
I can depict him married to the girl
Who in one breath rejected me because
She doubted I had talent to succeed.
It still hurts even now when I recall
Attempting to persuade her she was wrong."

    "That's good," was her reply, her voice clear as
A soaring flute, "those are the details that
Your brother wants included in your book —
Details in which your lives are intertwined

So nobody can tell whose life is whose.
What children then will you invent for him?
Will they be more successful than yours are?
Will they attend him as his sickness grinds
To its grotesque, inevitable end?"
　　　　She seemed caught up in asking questions such
As these, but then an upsurge blast of wind
Spread her cape out to signal her the time
Had come to leave. I felt relieved, the wind
Had chilled my bones, she was encroaching on
My privacy; uncannily, she seemed
To reach inside my thoughts as if she were
Aware of things I barely understood.
I wondered in my spinning mind if she
Was improvising what she chose to say
About my twin, describing him as ill;
Could she have thought that up in seeing me?
　　　　"I think you'd better leave," I said, "the wind
Is getting wilder now; the temperature
Will drop to zero when the moon is high."
My wife called out across the shaded room,
"Maybe she should remain with us tonight;
Invite her in, maybe she's lost her way."
There was more I could ask, I thought, although
Her cape kept pulling at her shoulder blades,
And I conjectured that I had choice
Of how to let her influence my book.
　　　　So there she is, still standing at my door.
That windy pause is where my book will end,
Giving me time to figure out what ought
To be included there, depending on
How much I need this brother in my life

To make it more complete, depending on
What I can do for him to help him bear
The illness of his final days, his thoughts,
As his white face, from chin, to mouth, to cheeks,
To eyes, comes closer to resembling mine.

PRIDE AND LAUGHTER

I am a primatologist; I do
believe humans are just creatures, too, special
only in that we know ourselves as such.
At our research compound, which simulates
their native habitat in Africa,
we study chimpanzees in social groups.
        My young wife, carrying our infant son,
his face squinched up into a round-eyed stare,
joined me to watch the romping chimpanzees
at raucous play: to our astonishment,
Mimi, who recently had given birth,
came to the fence and held her infant up
in ostentatious, proud display before
my beaming wife as if proclaiming that
"Our mother bond transcends our differences."
        I felt left out, for what, indeed, had I
to boast about of such significance?
But serendipity prevailed that day.
Coco, an adolescent male, had watched
these mothers showing off, and secretly
he filled his mouth with water and approached
the chain-link fence where we still stood, a look
of somber import in his steady eyes;
he leaned as close to me as he could get,
drew in a mighty breath through his wide nose,
then squirted the held water in my face.
        He paused to guess what my response would be,
and when I showed not anger but surprise,

he rolled upon his back, kicking his legs,
and started the pant laugh that chimpanzees
are famous for. Laughter is contagious,
as you well know, and so my laughing made
him laugh the harder and soon both of us
were uncontrolled hysterical, bonded
by our shared understanding of his joke.
  We males had found our own identity —
a little trivial, perhaps, compared
to sacred motherhood, but not to be dismissed
within the universal scheme of things —
or so says science in asserting what
we humans are, in search of dignity,
what we can honorably do between
our making babies and just having fun.

THE ECSTASY

I followed those four chimpanzees across
The tangled forest floor for half a day —
That's what I do, observe, describe — to see
Where they were headed for on what, I guessed,
Was territory still unknown to them,
Where they might find a solitary chimp
From some outlying tribe who'd wandered by
To browse, so they could corner him, tear off
His testicles and leave him there to bleed
Slowly to death. That is what we know now
Primate raiding parties do; that's how they deal
With their competitors for food and sex,
Although our anthropologists, for years,
Chose to believe that only humans showed
Such warlike violence. But no, it's part
Of our inheritance, going way back
Beyond what written history recalls.
Then suddenly the forest opened out
Onto a precipice of rocks beyond
Which tumbled down a waterfall, its spume
Catching the blazing midday sun and making
Little rainbows everywhere. The chimps,
Stunned by the sight, stopped absolutely still,
Transfixed, hair on their necks upright and stiff.
To my astonishment, one threw his arms
Up in the dazzling air, soon followed by
The next until all arms were waving as
They leapt around each other in a dance.

No doubt about it, they were worshipping
The waterfall in something very like
Religious ecstasy, and I was awed
By their capacity for awe; I was
A creature wondering at wondering.
In that illuminated interval
Those raiding chimpanzees wholly forgot
The mission they'd embarked upon, lost in
Their rapture at the waterfall, and I,
The watcher there, enraptured too, aware
Of the millennia that brought me here,
Aware of murder that they could forget,
Wished only that I could be one of them.

THE KING'S DILEMMA

When he espied her in the marketplace,
Her basket frugally replete, her hair
Pulled tightly back into a braid, her eyes
Cast downward in true modesty,
The widowed king — his first wife owned and ran
A candy store — fell instantly in love,
And would have then and there proposed to her,
But for his fear that she might choose
To marry him because he was a king.
What could he do? He could return disguised,
Say, as a carpenter, and woo the maiden
From emotions he so deeply felt.
But what if he persuaded her with sighs,
With promises of lifelong faithfulness,
With swoonings of unquenched desire, and she
Inevitably learned he really was
A king who lied to her, would she not have
To turn him down for his deceit, given
The expectations of her innocence?
Was it impossible, the king opined,
For power to be joined with poverty?
And so the king's advisors recommended
He read Kierkegaard to see if he
Could help the king unravel his dilemma
Of position and intent. He found
That the philosopher regarded kingship
Merely as a metaphor for God,
Rather than yearning flesh and urgent blood —

A God who had Himself to figure out
How humans might reciprocate His love
Without mistrusting it. Puzzling, he thought,
And even worse, the maiden symbolized
The human soul, its longing to transcend itself.
Something vaguely obscene, it seemed to him,
About this parable, it didn't fit;
He had no meaning other than himself,
An ordinary guy but for his wealth,
With one failed marriage that caused bitterness,
And, although beautiful beyond the norm,
The maiden was a woman, nothing else,
Not to be overly idealized
He warned himself from past experience,
Attractive for her worldly attributes.
   It's true, he loved her in the worst of ways.
"To hell with it," he thought, acknowledging
The swelling in his royal britches was
A resurrection of the sort he understood.
Still, he was flattered by the wild analogy,
Comparing him to God, a parable
In which he means more than he wants to mean
Or needs in order to give his desire
A purpose to fulfill itself for what it is.
   When he approached her in the marketplace,
Wearing his velvet cape with ermine trim,
He instantly declared his burning love,
Explaining how he'd had to overcome
His insecurity, and there was just
A fleeting moment's pause before she smiled,
Sweetly accepting his proposal as
She asked, "Have you been reading Kierkegaard?"

GRIZZLY PRAYER

Yes, I believe you when you tell me that
you have concern for my immortal soul;
you want to know how I can possibly
face death, death lasting for eternity,
with no faint expectation, not a twinge
of yearning hope for an earned afterlife
achieved through good works or through pious prayer.
  Here's why: during my recent surgery
my heart stopped for a second; when I woke,
there on my chest I saw the raw round circle
where the doctor zapped me back to life
with an electric shock. I'd seen no light
serenely, softly beckoning to me
when for that instant I was dead, nor did
I hear a Bach chorale to welcome me
to a more peaceful realm. But I'll recount
my most miraculous experience:
When hiking up a path in Glacier Park,
adding a white-winged crossbill to my list,
I was astonished when a bear lunged out
from right behind a huckleberry bush;
he stood immense on his hind feet as I,
without intent, blurted "Oh God!" out loud.
  The stream I walked beside then ceased to flow,
the leaves on the grey aspens went stone still,
dark clouds turned luminescent in dark sky,
three ravens stood transfixed on one stiff bough,
and in that instant's stillness God appeared.

"You atheists are all alike," God said,
"when trouble comes you call on me for help,
but I don't mind, it's just what I expect."
I was chagrinned, of course, and didn't want
to disavow my skeptical beliefs,
but God continued soothingly: "Here's what
I'm going to do," He said in His base voice,
"I'll turn this bear into a Christian bear,"
and pointing with His finger as immortal
Michelangelo depicted him,
God had the grizzly clasp his paws together
in the gesture of a holy prayer
and — this, I fear, may strain credulity —
the creature spoke distinctly as you hear
me speaking now. I never will forget
his piety: "Oh, Lord," said he, "I want
to thank You for this meal I'll now receive
as blessing from the bounty of Your hands."
	But as the bear was looking heavenward,
I bolted with more speed I'd ever dreamed
my legs possessed, and scuttled down the path
with bramble cuts and bruises on my shins,
the scene behind me just a blur, the clouds
reshaping in the sky, and that is why I
have agreed to meet you here beneath
this ancient tree, to share my puzzlement:
What shall I wish for in behalf of needful
creatures of the earth who live by prayer?

THE RABBI'S SPIEL TO HIS CONGREGATION

After three days of unrelenting rain
my bottom floor was flooded and I had
to move upstairs. The sheriff and his deputy
arrived in their rowboat, equipped with just
an outboard motor; they informed me that
I was required to leave the premises.
"No way," said I, "God will resolve this as
it pleases Him, and I have always placed
my faith in the Almighty Lord."
                                        And yet
it kept on pouring, so I had to go
another story up; some bland official
from the state appeared in a sleek,
thunderous motorboat, proclaiming that the law
required me to evacuate.
                                        But no,
my faith in God demanded that I stay,
and stay I did, amused with thoughts of Noah
in his ark, and like the classical
Midrash interpreters, I entertained myself
with questions like: where were the animals
allowed to poop, problems arcane and yet
quite practical. But still the rains came down;
I had to move onto the roof until
a helicopter came and told me through
a megaphone, I absolutely had
to leave at once. My faith prevailed, and yet

the littered waters rose, and so, of course,
I drowned.
        The next thing I recall was standing
on a line, waiting my turn to voice
my disenchantment to the Lord. "I kept
my faith in You, and You abandoned me,"
said I with chutzpah quite Promethean.
"Schlemiel! Stiff-necked schlemiel!" cried red-faced God,
laughing His rousing laugh divine, "I sent
a helicopter and two motor boats!"
        I slapped my head. "Dummkopf!" I shouted
to myself. I should have realized that God
performs His miracles through worldly means,
not by suspending nature's laws; and that's
the lesson God engraved upon my mind.
Then He returned me here (by helicopter,
not by any fancy means) to speak,
attending friends, to you, and tell His joke.
        You ask where in the Pentateuch the Lord
reveals His humor or His irony —
well, everywhere you look if you look in
the spirit of what helps our tribe endure.
Here's one example among multitudes:
providing Sarah with a son when she
is long past menopause; for irony,
naming him Isaac, which means laughing one;
can't you imagine the astonished eyes
bulging out in papa Abraham's pale face?
        Example two: when God declared to Moses,
"I show my mercy unto those to whom
my mercy shows, and I show grace to those

to whom my grace is shown." Hilarious
evasiveness, I'd say, a joke, a joke divine,
whose meaning lies in what we make of it.
    But I can't answer any more such questions
since my time is up, and you can hear
above the rising tides of fervent prayer
the whir of blades reflected in the sun —
my helicopter waiting on the roof.

REDESIGNED

Demonstrating that we can reverse the aging process
in [a rat] that shares 99 percent of our genes will
profoundly challenge the common wisdom that aging
and death are inevitable.
  — Ray Kurzweil, *The Singularity Is Near*

This thou perceiv'st that makes thy love more strong,
To love that well which thou must leave ere long.
  — William Shakespeare, sonnet #73

  What if Ray Kurzweil's prophecy is right
so that our children will be able then
to redesign their bodies and renew themselves,
thus making us the last in history,
the generation at the human edge,
constrained by our biology,
fated to age, evolved to die?
  Shakespeare believed
mortality makes precious what
we must relinquish in the name of love,
that our humanity's enlarged by loss,
shared sorrow sounds our deepest harmony.
If this heartbreakingly is true,
would a mild summer's afternoon
with languid clouds and lunch upon a lawn
in conversation with one's wife
about one's children's going forth
be emptied of the poignance that
awareness of mortality possessed
when time was running out on us,
when choice invested time

with singular significance —
one face beloved among a multitude,
one history to share?
     I do not want to age or die,
but neither do I wish to live forever
without urgency or tears,
transformed into a deity
who lives forever without consequence.
Although I'm curious to see
what happens next, then after that
and so on till the sun collapses on itself
to bring the human saga to an end,
I do not wish for immortality,
though I do wish the Bard of transience
walked alive among us still.
     But who can get his mind
around the thought of ageless youth
so alien to how our genes
have fashioned us: to be survivors
only through our mortal children's lives?
     Even in this vexed inquiry,
this groping in the humanly unthinkable,
this flicker in the noon
of who I am and who, no doubt,
my father was, and so on back into
the mist of origins, I question how
my redesigned inheritors
might well remember me, someone
who clings to summer warmth
while watching a careening bee
seeking the nectar of a flower,
his temporary moment in the sun.

III. MEDITATIONS AND FOREBODINGS

MEDITATION OF A JEW

A Jew myself, I hope
the Jews in Israel destroy
the terrorists in Lebanon
despite my more impersonal philosophy
that "alle Menschen werden bruder"
as Beethoven engraved that sentiment
deep in my heart
in his 9th symphony.
     Music — if only humankind could
reinvent itself though music
at its most exalted and sublime
and we could beam out Bach and Mozart,
Brahms and Beethoven
into the farthest galaxies,
proclaiming we're a peaceful species,
worthy of their trust,
to other forms of life
who've mastered hatred, ended war,
through willed intelligence
and they'd be safe to visit us.
     But trapped on crowded earth
which now seems like no more
than just an acre to be shared,
I can't escape the thought
terrorist hate exists beyond a cause,
beyond the explanations that
probing psychology provides,
and thus, I fear, beyond control:

they hate because they hate,
that goes for hating children too,
as they have done
for nearly two millennia.

This is the best that I can do
in trying to explain
what seems just inexplicable,
including killing in the name of God,
and I can find no hope and no
redeeming music in belief like this;
I must throw up my hands,
although I know prayer is in vain.

I tell myself my hatred
follows only from their hate;
I claim we have a basic right
to live accepted and in peace.
Is that too difficult
for human nature to achieve despite
what cutthroat history reveals,
going way back to when
we were ax-wielding tribes?
And yet "Choose life that you may live!"
the grieving Yahweh said to Moses,
thus implying that a choice,
a blessed choice, is possible.

The rubble, mixed with blood,
torn flesh, and splintered bones,
glitters right now in noonday sun
as if some natural catastrophe,
an earthquake, a volcano,
or an asteroid colliding with the earth —
some force indifferent

to human suffering —
caused devastation so extreme,
and yet was only nature
doing what it does without intent,
with no wish to do harm.
Yes, that would be believable.

      But maybe it's the Devil's work,
a Devil, entertained by spectacle,
despising Bach and Beethoven,
a watcher of TV, reader of newspapers,
a weapons connoisseur,
maybe this is his work.
Ah yes, though seemingly incredible,
this makes persuasive sense;
it just can't be that we
would do this to ourselves!

MOSES

Caught up between the stiff-necked multitude,
Exhausted and complaining, and his God,
Blasted by desert wind and sand and sun,
Lips parched and cracked, Moses called out for help,
Imploring Yahweh please to intervene
Since hostile Nature lay in His control.
      "Speak to the boulder," Yahweh said, "it will
abundantly bring forth fresh water for
Your people and their flocks." So Moses took
His rod and tapped the boulder twice, and lo!
A spring gushed out to slake each thirsty throat;
The people cheered — it was a miracle!
      But then to everyone's astonishment,
Yahweh, now furious at Moses and
His brother Aaron, now accusing them
Of lack of trust because they failed to do
Exactly as He said — speak to the rock,
Not tap it with a rod — decreed that they
Would die without their ever entering
The honeyed land He'd promised to them all,
The stiff-backed, wide-eyed people gathered there.
      Incredible! For such a small offense,
So petty and so technical, Yahweh
Denied to Moses — his true favorite,
As if he were old Yahweh's chosen son,
The one He talked to face to face — reward for trials
Moses had endured, from Pharaoh's wrath,
To terror at a voice that gave commands

Out of a burning bush, to isolation on
A mountaintop of thunder where new laws
Were given to augment His covenant.
        So what sense can I make of this? Can such
A father God be jealous of a man
He's loved as if he were His son? Is this
Why all creation's Lord forbade the fruit
Which would confer upon a human eater
Immortality and thus drove Adam
From the Garden into wilderness?
Is this the same Creator who renewed
His covenant by telling awestruck Moses
Just before his death that "I, your God,
Will circumcise your heart" to make His laws
No longer seem imposed, but feel as if
They now were part of nature as it is?
And is this God the one who in the name
Of holy love offered to Moses yet
A final choice between His blasting curse
Or blessing, death or life, advising him,
Exhorting him, "So now choose life!"
        And stiff-necked like the rest, how can I hold
The two together in my mind — a judge
Who is accuser and protector both,
Both coldly punishing and merciful?
Or is my questioning just angry rant,
As if I, too, were an abandoned son
Who can't accept blind nature as it is,
Whose wisdom is confused uncertainty,
Who has no comfort he can give to friends,
Whose consolation offers nothing but
A barren boulder in the desert wind?

Where are you now old father of the laws
We need as guides if we can choose to live,
Now as imploring tender throats are cut
And bombs fall on the innocents who sip
Cool drinks still hopeful in the bright cafes?

DARWIN'S BEETLE

With my new hip I'm able now to walk —
I am not finished yet — and so I hiked
Out to the woods to test my stamina,
But, sad to say, I tired and had to rest.
As I sat down on a decaying log,
My hand descended on a beetle which
I placed upon my palm to contemplate
The bond I share with other living things.
    As a young man, Darwin would walk into
The countryside to seek rare beetles he
Could add to his collection: one clear day
He came across two beetles, snatched them up
And headed briskly home, pleased with himself,
A beetle in each hand, to mount them each
According to its color, size, or form.
    On his way back, eyes down, he spied still yet
Another specimen not seen before
And hotly was compelled to capture it;
But since both hands were occupied, he put
One wildly squirming beetle in his mouth
To free a hand, but yuck! the beetle then
Excreted something acrid on his tongue,
And Darwin had to spit it out; repulsed,
He dropped a beetle from his hand to clasp
His burning mouth, and he returned with just
One specimen as trophy for the day.

That episode took place some years before
He sojourned forth to the Galapagos
Where he collected untold multitudes
Of specimens, of subtle variants,
Finches that differed just according to
The sizes of their beaks. And there his first
Great revelation of how things evolved
Through struggle or eventually died out
Began to take shape in his thoughts, although
He never did forget the day the angry
Beetle fouled his tongue and thwarted him.

    Imagining how Darwin felt — as if
It were my own experience — I taste
The panicked beetle's desperate excreta
Darwin spat out in disgust that day,
Saving itself from its apparent fate
Of being pinned to represent a blink
In nature's purposeless experiment
Of hungry life competing with itself.

    As I displayed the beetle in my palm,
And I beheld its shimmering, I thought
I could imagine its dire point of view
Equally well, how on returning home
The beetle's entry in its diary
Might have recounted its horrendous day:
"A monster put me in his mouth and tried
To eat me but I managed to escape;
I'm a survivor and my fertile seed
Will surely take dominion of the earth."

And so, no doubt against the scripted rules
Of struggle for one's progeny alone   -
Written in every palpitating cell,
I caught my breath, stood starkly up,
And flicked the cringing beetle from my palm
To send him on his inconclusive way.

BREAKING NEWS

In Baghdad yesterday a terrorist
blew himself up and killed nearly one hundred
ordinary people lined up hoping
to be hired for some construction jobs.
They took the risk of standing there to feed
their families. Against whom did the anger
from their widows' grief direct itself?
What worldly sense could they have made of this?
    In paradise a brown-eyed virgin was
assigned to greet the martyr and reward
his sacrifice. I wonder if she would
select this same man if she had the choice
under some other circumstance. How can
her role in this be understood if one
looks from her point of view? There is so much
involved, so much to take into account.
    Two hundred rockets rained on Israel
not caring whom they hit; no one was hated
in particular. Indifferent,
they seemed beyond blame like a hurricane,
just part of nature as it's always been.
There's nothing new here for the Jews; they've known
such wrath for two millennia. No man
who's capable of reason will assume
that hate will have some other end besides
long-prophesized apocalypse. Would Jews
be better off, I wonder, if they, too,
believed in some consoling afterlife?

There is so much to take into account:
passions, theologies, assumptions, facts.
          A girl, just eight years old, was raped, tortured,
buried alive. I can't imagine what
went through her mind. Perhaps we could explain
one part of this if we were certain that
the rapist was abused as a small child.
Should some small portion of our sympathy
go out to him? Was he neglected or
unloved? So much remains obscure, so much
is hidden in unfathomable dark.
          Four days ago our cat got out the door,
but she did not return as she had done
so many times before. Baffled, dismayed,
I looked for her down by the stream, thinking
she'd need to drink; I looked for her within
the aspen grove, thinking she might feel safe
within its shade; I looked for her along
the meadow's edge — maybe she might catch voles
to keep herself alive. Only by chance,
by luck, I found her miles away last night
in a deserted owl-infested barn.
Perhaps she got confused or thought I had
abandoned her. So much uncertainty —
always so much to take into account.
          Who knows what her fate would have been if I
had not arrived in time to rescue her?

ACADEMIC PARTY

I was invited to a cookout at
a colleague's country house to celebrate
the ending of the academic year
with lots of people that I didn't know —
an opportunity to chat with scholars
teaching other disciplines than mine.
I told a young biologist the thesis
of my recent book on Shakespeare is
that characters who seem immutable
in their identity can be transformed,
miraculously it would seem, by choice,
an act of will that comes from who knows where —
like Edmund, the arch-villain in *King Lear*
who, just before his death, proclaims, "Some good
I mean to do in spite of mine own nature,"
though swift time runs out before he can
save Lear's good daughter from his own command
that she be hanged. My puzzled colleague
grudgingly replied that he could not explain
a transformation so complete, without
some antecedent cause, with knowledge he
possessed; "People are always what they are,"
his certitude proclaimed, and he walked off
to join a conversation at the bar.
Abundant food was served to sanctify
the year of our accomplishments, seeking
new knowledge and new truths: grilled salmon steaks,
a loin of pork, a roast of venison.

The hours passed by quite pleasantly
since I was in my party haze, and then
at coffee time a group, unknown to me,
assembled in a circle by a hedge
of lilac bushes coming into bloom.
Our country's policies abroad emerged
predictably as topics for debate;
I listened as I'd learned to do, although
I'd heard these selfsame views expressed before.

       One man — I never found out who he was
although he wore slick lizard boots — held forth:
"In Israel," he said, "the ruling men
all beat their wives and rape their daughters in
their kosher homes." Hardly believing what
my ears took in, I looked around the circle
where dessert was balanced on each knee,
expecting someone would dispute the man's
astonishing remark — or so it seemed
to me, the only Jew attending there,
but no one spoke a disapproving word,
as if his claim might be believable.

       After a pause, I challenged him: "Would you
have made such an outrageous claim
if you had known a Jew is present here?"
Did he assume, I asked my inner self,
that anyone would find him credible?
Did he subscribe to that old forgery
that Jews were plotting to control the banks
and thus control the world? He looked at me,
but he did not reply; he just got up
and disappeared among a chatting crowd,
only his lizard boots remaining in

the confines of my memory. Still worse,
no blank-eyed colleague there came up to me
to sympathize for the affront that they
surely had recognized as such. They sipped
their final sips and silently they too
dissolved among the mingling celebrants.
      "What shall I make of this bizarre event —
the faceless lizard-man's horrendous words,
the silence of complicit bystanders,"
I asked myself. "Shall I consider it
a lie of choice or choicelessness? What more
might I have done? Should I inform my hosts
as they shake hands with their departing guests?
I'm sure they'd be aggrieved and mortified."
But I decided NO — no good could come
from my humiliating them. My choice
was just to let the matter go, though one
can see that choice still festers in my mind.
      As I walked to my car to drive back home,
my wife's assuring arm locked tight in mine,
I noticed Venus had just risen in
the western sky — an observation that
a literary man like me might well
enjoy for its ironic contrast with
the hatred I had just endured, the lie
of hate that loves itself — as if I lived
within a poem where blind insanity
was shown for everyone to recognize.
      But not that night. Better the sun's eclipse;
better an ice storm cracking branches down
upon the roofs of sleeping families,
of dreaming fathers, mothers, daughters, sons,

on everyone who does not know, and does not wish to know, exactly what is wrong, though some must choose to realize as they wake to the world that something terrible has happened and is happening.

RAIN IN AUGUST

I have had some success before, so I'm
Inclined to try again. During the drought
I prayed for rain last summer and it rained.
Here's what I figure is deducible
from that result: just modest prayers will
sometimes be granted only if one prays
to the right god. My fixed assumption is
that one must never overreach, and thus
cautious restraint and modesty remain
essential to my strategy. One can't
pray only for oneself, although it would
be hypocritical pretending one
had nothing personal at stake — no god
would fail to see through such a blatant ruse.
    So following these rules, I prayed for rain,
not everywhere on earth where crops are dry,
or even everywhere throughout the state —
I feared that would be overreach — only
right here in this vicinity. Right here
there are enough fruit orchards, ranches, farms,
resorts catering to clientele who like
their vistas green, to make a neighborhood.
    My model was the biblical Elijah
who had challenged all the priests of Baal
to supplicate their phony god for rain
with the ironic touch that maybe Baal
was sleeping and thus couldn't hear their cry.
"So call him louder!" was Elijah's taunt,

sex causes jealousy, mistrust, and hurt
that comes from differing dependencies.
Mothers and fathers equally will do
the necessary nurturing; why should
male breasts be wasted and not put to use?

      Surely there's too much grief and suffering —
more human kindness is the cure for that —
though sorrow seems to deepen us in doses
small enough to bear and overcome.
But I'm uncertain what to recommend
about mortality. That's tough because
I can't imagine how eternity
might be arranged to work. What age
or time of life should be made permanent?
Too much preoccupation with oneself
when one is young disqualifies youth as
the right condition for eternity;
and, strangely, I would not want to forgo
the melancholy of declining age,
the soothing air of slow forgetfulness.

      Maybe I need to give more thought to this;
      Maybe I'd better only ask for rain.

assuming they were praying to a god
who wasn't there at all, did not exist.
Let me repeat myself: one should not pray
to any deity who doesn't care —
of which there seem to be an awful lot —
or one without sufficient power to grant
a reasonable wish, a sage request.

       Maybe my modest prayer was merely luck;
that is, of course, a possibility
I should have mentioned from the start.
What person with the smallest speck of reason
in his head would not consider that?
The gods may be constrained by principles
of quantum randomness, but how this works
is barely comprehensible to me.

       Then in a thunderclap this thought occurred
that my entire strategy was wrong:
if one prays to a minor god one gets
minor results. And so I asked myself,
had anyone gone all the way and wished
for total change, conditions on the earth
completely different from what they are?
Such prayer might have immense appeal to an
aspiring god with pity in his heart.

       So here's my new list of requests, hopi
THE major god will like my propositions
and will then resolve to try them out:
First, eating's got to go. You can't have life
depending on the taking of some other life
creatures must be designed to thrive only
on water and on air. Then, sex between
a man and woman has to be revised;

MOUNTAIN MEDITATION

The snow-topped mountain range
across the eastern sky,
electric blue as dusk comes on —
that is the view I've chosen
now that old age shapes my needs,
the view my study window
in the house we had our son design
looks out upon as if it were
an inner view into myself as well.
Late winter afternoons
sunlight upon the heaped-up snow
transforms the blazing white to blazing pink,
then darkens into purple
with its own internal glow.
Indifferent, austere, spectacular,
devoid of meaning to console
upon which I can meditate, I dwell
upon the human history of cruelty,
so vast that it defies depiction, yet
I still believe somehow
ultimate destruction might be
avoidable, controlled
by kindness, what at best we are, unlike
tornados, floods, or hurricanes,
earthquakes, and epidemics, accidents.
But surely what I wish cannot be true,
hatred and war, vindictiveness,
must be as much a part of nature

as the seasons are,
and even if a lawful god designed it so,
I cannot worship him;
I won't allow myself to long
for immortality of any kind —
even a universe
where in some obscure place
pulsating life can make itself at home.
I close my eyes and picture suns
collapsing and extinguishing themselves
in space that thins to nothingness;
I see a summer cricket silenced
beneath his once protecting stone.
And yet I am consoled, at least in part,
or partly so, by late vermilion light
now changing on the mountain peaks,
because I choose to make this spectacle
signify what I am,
because for now it's here,
as you and I are here — as if that's all
we need to know, trembling together
in the impersonal, chill air
of the transfigured mountain's afterglow.

FLOURISHING BIRCHES

Eight seasons after I had planted them
to complement the evergreens —
cedars and spruce and firs and pines
that dominate this mountain landscape
in Montana where we dwell —
these glowing birches thrive
just with the aid of watering
(and pep-talk flattery from me)
reaching above the soaring chimney
of our hewn-log home.
    A stranger cannot tell
I've given teeming nature
this transfiguring assist;
the chickadees approve
since now they have smooth branches,
free of prickly needles,
they can rest upon
while taking feeder turns
(my bounty always keeps it full)
which in their thankful minds
must seem miraculous.
    But here's the rub. What if
a deity who's inexperienced
at fabricating worlds —
with this one his first try —
whose special pride is
improvising evergreens,
suggesting life has power to endure,

might understandably be vexed,
thinking I'm interfering with his own
preferred original design?
      Though there are weather zones
that set a limit to the range
where trees can grow within
their designated boundaries,
not every tree that can survive this cold
will be found flourishing
in this zone where we've made our home.
Maybe that is because the deity,
familiar with his balmy realm,
just wants to have his way,
and if he's mad enough,
he well could lay a curse, a blight,
upon the land to make sure
his displeasure is well understood.
We've seen such blight wherever
humans settle in.
      But here's the reasoning
my own delight in trees prefers:
I think the world was organized
intentionally incomplete
so we could add to it,
collaborate in the creation
with a friendly deity, one
open-minded, not competitive,
and thus enjoy a sense
of shared and mutual ownership
we both can celebrate.
      And yet much evidence
suggests this cheerful view

may not be accurate:
an inexperienced creator —
(what did he do before he went to work?)
having conceived of trees for shade
and for the virtuoso shapes of leaves,
their moody movement in the wind —
might well foresee pleasure
could quickly turn to greed for property,
and property could lead
to fighting over ownership.
Perhaps our inclination to possess
clinches the case for leaving worldly things
exactly as they are
with evergreens and aspens quite
sufficient on this mountaintop.

      But birches fit this landscape
perfectly; no sensible deity
could possibly consider otherwise
or fail to join me in admiring
changing hues of yellow leaves
birches bestow to autumn air
in what feels like exuberance.

      So maybe there's a message
to be found in my uncertainty
of what to augment or to modify
and what to leave alone,
on how much pleasure is appropriate
for just a temporary world;
maybe I've got the deity all wrong
in how I have invented him walking
unblemished woods and fields of paradise
while contemplating trees

designed and suitable for earth;
maybe there's more I need to know
as I breathe in the chill autumnal air
of how to tend my little patch
of cultivated mountain land,
bestowing blessings on whatever trees
are able to survive
and can with care
be made to flourish and to grow.

WEDDING CEREMONY

      I still can see her in my freshman class,
self-possessed and always in control,
eager to try out her views, yet wary
not to intimidate her classmates by
revealing how much more she'd read than they,
how much she understood. And I can see her
on her wedding day, so luminous that I
could think that harmony might win
the ancient war against discord,
spirit and rebel body might be one.
      The only Jew among the many guests,
I'd driven half across the state
to read a poem that would contribute to
the ceremony she had modified
where stoic Shakespeare says
awareness of one's own mortality
can "make thy love more strong," a concept
we had shared through many afternoons
of worried talk.
      The wedding was arranged
to take place at her parents' mountain home
within a clearing between evergreens,
the folding chairs lined up in rows,
waiters efficiently replenishing
all snacks and drinks, everything organized;
but then a squall of unexpected rain
threatened to drive the wedding party
in the house against her father's will,

despite his incredulity that what
he planned might actually be thwarted
by a chance event.
               I still can picture how
the dark clouds parted and the sun appeared
as if determined by command; and thus
the threatened ceremony had begun.
Her grandfather, with great white eyebrows
and a matching beard, a curled forefinger
that seemed ready to reach out to touch,
sat right up front beside me since we both
were scheduled to recite a poem
before the minister began the legal part
that followed his uplifting words about
the holy spirit's presence there.
               But just as he had neared "I now pronounce,"
Grandpa's control gave out: he leaped
from his discarded chair right past the couple
and the minister and went behind a tree
to urinate as nature in that instant
had decreed. The setting sunlight added
dazzle to the golden arc he made,
his version of a rainbow-covenant with earth,
with frailty, with finitude, and he returned,
unfazed, a grin upon his face — or so
it seemed to me — back to his chair to hear
the minister's concluding words.
               Soon afterwards, the consummating message
having been bestowed, taking my turn
on their receiving line to shake the hand
of the ecstatic groom — the golden arc
still blazing in my dazzled mind —

waiting my turn on the receiving line,
I then leaned over to embrace the bride,
my doubting student, my inheritor,
who whispered in my heated, Hebrew ear:
"Where would I be without my grandfather?"

THE PEACEABLE KINGDOM

Despite my wobbly legs,
despite forgetfulness, old age is not
without its compensations — such
surprising ones as lowered levels
of testosterone. So mazel tov to me,
I am at last relieved
of the compelling need
to win and to compete,
and thus I can more readily
enjoy the triumphs
and successes of my friends
(though not my enemies —
I am not talking about miracles).
And lust, thank Yahweh, praised be he,
(I mean biology, of course)
has finally abated
and removed the need
to exercise control, day in, night out,
in order to remain true
to commitments and ideals.
Oy weh! What a relief!
How wonderful to be
master of my desires
or what remains of them,
concerned with sorrows
far beyond my own — a sentiment
for which I can admire myself
and yet remain within

the strictures of humility.
Ah, yes, humility, a word which means
composed of dust — the dust
to which we must return,
although we still insist
the chosen people is
what we have always been.
And now in my declining years,
for just a while, a promised interval,
Peaceable Kingdom, here I am —
I'll take my blessings as they come —
where lamb and lion do lie down
together out of sheer fatigue!

AFTERLIFE

After two years of being dead, my Mom
has not contacted me with information or
advice. That's not like her at all.
Perhaps she's sitting by a misty lake,
watching the sunrise mirrored
as the ripples reach the pebbled shore,
with her beloved sister whom she missed so much
in her own final years, talking about —
what else? — their kids.
No doubt she's still concerned,
but with a difference now — now she's detached
from what is still our suffering,
the grief we feel, and go on feeling, when
we contemplate their deaths. No, suffering
cannot be justified as needed to give
meaning to the world: whoever thought it wise,
it is a bad idea; no one can take
pain on themselves to help somebody else,
not even parents, husbands, wives;
not even the most sympathetic god.
So there they sit beside the lake
beneath a wafted willow tree,
its boughs lit up with goldfinches;
they're quietly content to be together
once again, but not so happy that
their happiness prevents them from remembering
that there is nothing they can do to make

their children's losses anything but what they are,
their own, yes, inescapably their own,
as I sit thinking here beside a misty lake,
watching the waves repeat themselves,
waiting for Mom to tell me what to do.

SURVIVAL

We need hope to survive, we need a goal
that's reachable on our own fragile earth,
acceptance of each other if not love,
stirred by the consolations art can bring,
remembering the sorrows we have seen,
remembering the harm we each have done.
Yet how impersonal our weapons are:
we cannot know who gets obliterated
in a flash; their childhoods and their loves
must be retold to make them permanent.
The TV broadcasts of whatever war
is in the news are meant to entertain
not to appall; we are not shown the face
of anguished death as Homer chanted it
to his awed listeners who understood
the irony that brash Achilles' shield,
made by a god, could not postpone his death
or bring his friend back from his crusty grave.
The storied past endures, and so I can
still picture when the Holocaust commenced:
the riots now recalled as Kristallnacht
for all the smashed-in doors and shattered glass
the Nazis and the looting citizens
strewed in the Jewish stores: the bakeries,
the groceries, the gleaming candy shops,
as neighbors grabbed whatever didn't burn,
their friendships wiped out in indifference
once thought unthinkable.

The Jews who saw
that worse was yet to come sought to escape,
although some stayed — the pianist Birkenfeld
who organized an orchestra in Lodz,
right in the ghetto's smoking heart, performed
Schubert and Beethoven, trying to cheer
the victims in discord as if they could
appeal, if not to absent God, at least
to rousing music that might still express
the hope for unified humanity.

But then the ovens of the Holocaust
occurred and these atrocities must be
recorded with the rest, though how dare one
speak openly of the unspeakable;
it happened and forever will remain
a part of human history for those
who choose not to forget. We all have seen
the spectral bodies bulldozed into graves,
nameless and irretrievable beyond
what power we have to grieve, beyond remorse,
beyond what sacred pity can reclaim.

And now at home, in my worn leather chair,
I'm listening enthralled to Beethoven
on speakers whose benign technology
can make the music sound as if I were
attending a live concert like the one
at death-defying Lodz, although some wish,
some incredulity, tells me I'm safe,
no swastiked police patrol the streets,
no missiles streak across the bludgeoned sky
toward Tel Aviv, Hebron, Jerusalem.

But if I'm wrong — the end will come, and if
it's thinkable that even memory
will not survive beyond that final flash,
I hope I will be able in that pause,
in that last instant, to compose myself
and turn the volume up to hear the swell
of Beethoven's Third Symphony, the chords,
contained as a crescendo in my mind,
defiant and triumphant chords that rise
and drift out in the silent emptiness
of unredeemable indifference.

CHOICE

In the decisive year he died,
an exile from his longtime home,
the year that World War II began,
Freud wrote of his great fear
that humankind with instruments
designed to kill like nothing else
previously conceived
(and this was still before
the atom bomb was dropped)
had finally achieved the power
to wipe out human life,
with not a moment left to write
the poems of remorse,
as if extinction were our deepest,
most collective wish.
        His lips and jaw set tight against
the cancer that afflicted him,
he wondered if the god of death —
whom he called Thanatos —
might have in this extreme provoked
his equally immortal adversary,
Eros, god of love,
to summon up new strength and will
in the defense of life,
just as the Hebrew god, in whom
the stricken Freud no longer could believe,
had warned the aged Moses:
people had to make a choice

whose consequence was either
to be cursed or blessed: "Choose life
that you may live," grim Yahweh said.

But how can Cupid's bow,
inconsequential when it comes to war,
contend against the weaponry
that human genius has produced?
Freud feared our hearts and minds
are fired by power to destroy.
What argument for sympathy
can win the case against historic
hatred hardened with the passion
to confirm and justify itself?

Sigmund, determined doctor
who would cure us of our guilt
for being what we are,
where would you put your faith right now
as we stand on a precipice beyond
even the brink you knew so well?
What anguish for our children's sake
do we have strength to build upon?
How can we reinvent our dreams?

How strange, how fleeting strange,
that I am asking this right now,
my own days dwindled to a few,
watching effulgent yellow
in the birch tree by my window
blaze in October light as if,
closing my eyes, I could
extinguish every thought but this —
the yellow leaves against
a hanging cloud, the cloud

streaked purple and streaked blue,
the breeze-stirred yellow leaves
unraveling the tree —
as if this image could be held
and be a balm, a consolation like
the white indifference of eternity.

CONUNDRUM

All right then, let's assume
modern cosmology is accurate,
astonishing though it may seem,
that there was neither time nor space
until Big Bang occurred;
nothing, a total void, prevailed —
if nothingness can be conceived
despite this palpable, fine word
that designates absence as absolute.
The laws of nature then commenced,
and only then a universe
of mass and energy began
its history of change, with change itself
both means and destiny.
        But whoa! Here is a whopping problem
and a mighty paradox
which can't escape our scrutiny.
How did this plasma soup of nature know
what laws it was determined to obey?
There has to be an abstract realm,
as Plato premised in his cave, in which
the laws of math abide, and always have,
before they entered into space and time.
Although not physical themselves,
these laws gave birth from nothingness
to unimaginably hot quarks,
controlling how they would combine,
becoming atoms and then molecules

as matter cooled and space expanded,
thus allowing me, in only
thirteen billion years or so, to strut
my strophes on this planetary scene.
　　And yet, how can such laws exist
before the medium in which they can exist
itself exists? I think, in thinking this,
in thinking the word "nothingness,"
I may have spun myself into a vertigo
in which thought can't contain itself,
in which thought thinks what can't be thought.
　　So what you have before you here
is an embodied, thinking poem,
and as a poem it therefore must convey,
according to fixed laws of poetry (my own),
not merely an idea, but how it feels
to savor an idea within a mind
that is not floating somewhere off in space,
but here, right here in howling winter by
a fireplace warming my tired bones,
yet not at ease for reasons that
my probing is not certain of:
maybe because there's so much
hatred out there for us Jews; maybe
because my grandson lives so far away.
　　But I'm not in a self-exploring mood
for meditating on the circumstances
of my life. Although it makes me feel
minutely insignificant —
one snowflake as a blizzard passes through —
I must admit I like to dwell
on cosmic mysteries; I like

the pure impersonality
of evolutionary narratives,
the very concept of causation, how
new transformations then transform
old transformations, wondering
what they are destined to achieve — perhaps
more consciousness among the galaxies,
perhaps more peace for humankind.
        A realm of numbers and equations
that's beyond what's merely physical,
beyond mortality, and grief, and loss,
a realm that theoretically cannot exist
whose laws we live by every day!
How absolutely baffling, my dear friend,
and elegant; how wonderful
and how appalling just to be right here
on whirling earth, warmed by a fire
and safe at least for now, today,
where I can think about such permanence
amid such vanishing, and have my say.

IV. LANDSCAPES AND SELF-PORTRAITS

IT'S MAY AGAIN

It's May again, and I'm still here to breathe
The wafted fragrance from the lilac bush
Because there's no work left for me to do,
My work is done; for better or for worse
I've finished what I would become, what I
Completed and have been, and so I'm free
To loiter in the fragrance of a lilac bush,
To feel the soothing sun as if its warmth
Were meant for consolation, meant for me.
The lilac bush, the streak of goldfinches
That glitter in their springtime hue — I'm here
To smell, to see, to meditate, no more
Strained laboring to be just what I am,
No urgency except to pause and watch
Goldfinches in their golden fluttering.
I'm here, I still am here, with nowhere else
To long for or to go; and so I listen
To the booming of an early bee
As if he, too, is happy that it's May
Right here on earth, ready for what a bee
Needs to be ready for, and so I say
I'm ready to remain here longer in
The lilac air, to breathe the scented light
Of what remains of this remaining May.

BUTTERFLY

"What comes out orange in the morning and
is very bright?" the earnest teacher asked
her kindergarten class, to which my son
replied, "A butterfly." He was marked WRONG,
and at our interview she said "Perhaps
he's not quite ready to be learning at
the kindergarten level." Her answer,
SUN, was just too obvious for him;
I pictured her transformed as punishment
Into a slug beneath a rotting log.
This story soon became a treasured part
of family mythology; my son
began to take delight in it, and so
when summer came, he lay down in the field
one blazing noon and placed a little dish
of sweetened water on his forehead as
he waited for a butterfly to land.
Behold, one did — my laughing son had been
anointed by a monarch butterfly;
at my suggestion, though reluctantly,
he chased and captured it. Urged on by me,
he mounted it on cotton under glass
in a carved frame engraved with antique gold.
His teacher praised him roundly for his care
in saving it, but on my birthday he
presented it to me; I hung it right
above my desk, and there it has remained
for all these half-attentive years, glowing

and undiminished in a misty longing
to believe in something permanent.
The night I got the phone call from my son
that I was now a grandfather — a wish
I'd dreaded never might come true — I had
one of those super-vivid dreams in which
the dawning sun appeared as if it were
a giant monarch butterfly whose wings
caused wind to stir and lift astonished leaves,
disturbing the sleek surface of the lake
with whitened swirls and foaming crests. And when
I woke, still shivering and feverish,
I saw an endless undulating stream
of butterflies all navigating south,
orange and black against the cobalt sky,
as if they suffered no uncertainty
of what was lasting right or lasting wrong,
or where they'd chosen to be heading to.

TAMARACKS

Now comes the turning of the tamaracks,
The only evergreen to lose its needle-leaves,
From yellow-gold to gold to golden bronze
And their reflections which the lake retrieves.

And I am wondering if pleasure from the past,
Which soon of course these sights will be,
Brings sadness in the knowledge that they're gone
Or restoration in their memory.

Do I see what is there as there? Or is
My sense of modulating light so strong
That gold already now seems bronze,
And even naming bronze as bronze seems wrong.

Yet there they are, I see them in their glow;
I see them doubled in the lake
As if my eyes, unlike my shifting mind,
Are of this world, and won't make the mistake

Of losing touch with happiness
By asking trees to give what they can't give —
Gold meaning or gold permanence —
But only live as ghostly colors live.

SPIDER

The first few yellow leaves, still on the tree,
Proclaim what is to come, like messengers.
But I have heard this message many times;
The future is exactly like the past
With autumn coming back, and so red leaves
And yellow leaves, though they delight my eyes,
Seem more like memory than prophecy —
As if I've been where I have yet to go,
And thus the present is enlarged for me.
      Though I had not expected it — and not
Within the realm of likelihood — a spider,
Dangling silently from silver thread,
Drops to the lowest yellow leaf as I'm
About to snatch it from the tree, as if
To claim that leaf to be his own. But why?
Surely his reasons are inscrutable
Like quantum randomness, which makes his motive
Like my whim — and that amuses me
And adds my laughter to the scene we share.
      Is it not true that humankind desires
To feel connected to this planet where
We try to make ourselves at home, not just
As chance survivors passing swiftly through
Some phase of evolutionary time,
But residents because we will it so
Since willing is what we've evolved to do?
      And thus I fancy that I'm bonded to
This miniature spider as we share

This flick of time, this space, this preference,
And I will let the yellow leaf remain
Unplucked upon the maple tree so that
He's free to spin his perfect web today
And he can do, as I myself have done,
Exactly what it is within his nature
He aspires to do, so that my watching
In this morning light may make us one.

IT'S ONLY WIND

It's only wind — clawed roots are strong enough
To keep tall trees upright — not a tornado
Or a hurricane; I don't hear bulldozers
Or dynamite or bombs. The animals are safe
In caves, or underground, or in their nests.
It's only wind, and yet wind could grow worse,
Which something in me does anticipate,
Something perhaps that has to do
With what I am, what everybody is,
Something that always was and cannot change
Despite our efforts and our best intents.
What can it be in us that's bent
On ripping, smashing. breaking, causing pain,
Just like streaked winds stirred to a storm
That has no consciousness or choice
Except to be exactly what it is
Without remorse or sympathy that we
Are born to learn and comprehend.
Yet even sympathy gives way to wind,
Wind of our own devising, wind of hate,
As if the children in the street are threats to us
And must be stopped before they're big enough
To take revenge for previous revenge?
I hear the widow's voice now tuned to grief;
I see blank faces of the passive poor;
The thief feels safe in the dark alleyways;
The liar counts his money in the bank.
But I will not put up with it; I won't allow

Our nature to continue being what it is
As if the lashing winds are just the same
As you and I, yes, you, my ancient enemy.
I'll hold my groping blind hand out until
We both confront our unrelenting hearts;
If we embrace, my dagger poised to thrust
Into your back, and yours to thrust in mine,
Maybe at last, appalled, we will take heed,
Remaking what we have been made, though wind
Uproots tall trees as it has always done.

BEAR GRASS

Here in northwest Montana in the spring
Blooms a big flower — bear grass is its name
Because bear eat the fleshy leaf sheaths after
Winter sleep has much depleted them.
They bloom in intermittent years, stark white,
Composed of a dense pulsing multitude
Of tiny petals like a galaxy —
Or so it pleases me to think of them.
      Yet each third year or so, they manage to
Coordinate, another thought I like
To contemplate, appearing all together
As a tidal surge in unison
And fill the forest with a scented glow,
Eerie as moonlight on a cloudless night.
      They are extravagantly beautiful —
No one could possibly think otherwise!
So maybe watching this effulgent scene
Should be considered happiness because —
Although I add my thoughts to what I see —
It is impersonal, thus capable
Of helping one forget true sorrows one
Must call one's own — sorrows that signify
The story of one's only life, events
Already fixed and inescapable:
A blank-faced parent's loss of memory,
Desertion by a longtime trusted friend,
A child's prolonged disease and death. Such thoughts
Cannot for long be banished from the mind.

But who says only happiness that lasts
Can be considered happiness at all?
And who says we're designed for happiness?
So watching bear grass this white spring, even
For just an hour, in which they bloom as if
Delighting in each other's company,
Will have to be enough and must suffice
As happiness. I will it so, and so
It is until unknown events contrive
To take me somewhere I don't want to go;
And may the bears soon satisfy their needs
Where they can pause and eat and stay alive.

SPRING RAIN

Lush and luxurious, the maple leaves,
after light rain, illuminate themselves,
or so it seems to such a watcher as
I've been and am, who is astonished still,
still wondering grim circumstance has not
changed everything I love — the look of leaves,
the way my looking looks to me as if
I stood outside myself and could perceive
my shaded self illuminated by
the glow reflected from the maple leaves.
A northern oriole alights upon
an upper branch as if his instinct wish
is to give focus to the scene, as if
he knows my mind will welcome and absorb
each luscious image earth provides, so I
can make what's lush into what's lusher still
by adding what is most impersonal
about myself, what grinding age has not
negated or destroyed — the simple gift
and unacquisitive delight of looking
at a world that didn't have to be.
And yet it is — a world that will not grieve
when no one's there to watch an oriole,
after warm rain in this remaining spring,
lift and depart in the quick silver light
of an illuminated maple tree
and disappear beyond imagining.

SLEEPY DOG BLUES

His body has begun to fail, my dog
of fifteen faithful years,
as mine, too, has begun to fail:
diminished eyesight, hearing dulled.

He twitches in his sleep,
pursued, perhaps pursuing, ready
to be aroused as in his lusty days,
though this may be my own
perverse imagining.

Yet he is spared the need to mourn
the loss of parents and of friends,
though when his sibling died
a year ago, companion to us both
throughout these vanished years,
I do believe he moped about the house
at least a month; but maybe I'm
projecting my own grief on him.

At least I know he is not tempted by
the strained illusion of an afterlife —
the curse that came unbidden when
our human consciousness evolved
and turned our one-time dying
into everlasting death,
death lasting through eternal time.

But now he jumps up on the couch,
rebel against my weak authority,
as he has always done,
(with just a little help from me),

and stretches out, absorbing
all the comfort that he needs
merely through touch, his nose
deliciously upon my lap,
still wet and cold, still cold and wet.
    It is as if his senses are
triumphant as they've always been, and wise,
and so I picture him tail up, still
undistracted and serene, sniffing along
the scented fields of paradise.

SUNRISE

The sun, about to rise into my sight,
makes the mute mountain's shadow
shudder in the lake, its trees
emerging greenly at their tips;
for just an instant sun rays seem to pause
as silhouettes of birds streak past,
too fast to be identified or cause
their names to take shape on my lips.

And then, with a titanic thrust,
the orange orb appears not yet too bright
for me to set my gaze upon
and watch blue silhouettes of fleeting birds
transfigured in the spreading light
become identifying words.

I must have stood here in this spot,
seeking conceivable serenity,
perhaps a thousand years ago,
or maybe only yesterday,
and witnessed what I witness now,
the mountain peak still patched with snow,
the glitter on the water as
white lilting waves lift up and sway.

And maybe I'll return tomorrow or
a thousand years from now,
to seek to reassure myself
that nothing changes in the way
light shapes the mountain's shadow
on the lake to start another day,

repeating what has gone before,
without elusive memory, content
with what is there and nothing more.
       But happiness, a moment's kiss
whose moisture holds a moment's breath,
now reawakens in my restless mind,
composed of pleasure vanished in a wisp,
ten leaves blown down to five, to two, to one,
like disappearing birds,
and so I stare at the emerging sun
that changes only to return to what
it was, to what I still can keep.
And when I'm ready with my words
to welcome some concluding sleep,
rocked by the pulsing wind upon the lake —
though I'm not ready yet —
perhaps I'll think there's nothing left for me
to mourn for, nothing for me to regret.

SUNFLOWER

Large luminescent yellow
outer petals in two undulating rows
serenely complement
the middle circle made of minute sepals
tightly clustered to suffuse
their own distinctive lemon hue.
Both circles are in perfect harmony
with pale green radiance
that flows from this bold flower's core
as if proclaiming to the universe,
"Observe me here, I'm beautiful!"
and in spontaneous response,
I blurt out, "Yes, oh Hallelujah, yes!"
assuming some acknowledgment
from me is certainly required here,
although I show restraint
and do not rub myself
against the flower's beckoning
to help it propagate itself
throughout the open spaces
out there in the glowing fields and hills.
The sexual dance is not the role
I'm given here; I leave that
to the insects and the birds,
certain the chickadees will eat
its nutrient and oily seeds
when they are ripe.

And so I am content to watch,
content to be a spectator.
    I think I understand
how evolution works, creating beauty
as incentive to make love,
but I am puzzled as to why
beauty — the thing enclosed
in the idea — emerged to be
admired for itself alone
so that all passion holds me here
without a propagating role to play,
only desire to observe.
    So, too, I understand why
our large brains evolved — so we
could learn how best to hunt
and where to find our sustenance
and how to get along with our own kind;
learning is practical,
it's what big brains do well.
But I cannot explain the leap
our species made in wishing to know things
just for the sake of knowing them.
Why do we need to know about black holes,
that there's a limit to how fast light goes,
or comprehend the painful facts
about ourselves — how we are thrilled by war,
how killing helps us to deny
our own mortality, the burden
of our unrelenting consciousness?
And what good does it do to realize
even our solar system must collapse
upon itself and meet its fiery end?

Bright flower of my choice, my own
by virtue of my loyalty,
have I abandoned you
by turning inward for an interval
as if my first allegiance must be to
what's in my mind? Well, once again,
I will renew my vow to watch
your colored circles, luscious yellow,
innuendo green, as if
they are the only certain world,
timeless, ongoing, and yet still,
a world in which I know myself
as if I were not here at all.

ILLUMINATION

A swirl of snow arrived last night —
Wet snow, the kind that clings to trees;
The forest is composed of light
This whitened dawn, and only these,

Silence and light, delineate
The laden pines, cedars, and firs,
Tall tamaracks. So I relate
Their glittering as it occurs,

Their saga of serenity,
Without words of embellishment,
Round phrases meant to rescue me
From what's to come, my dark descent.

Indeed, I am not needed here,
Nor does it matter where I go,
Or if new whiteness will appear,
Except to say that this is so.

OLD MAN WALKING

We could conceive that all the conditions for the first
production of a living organism [existed] in some
warm little pond . . . that a compound was chemically
formed ready to undergo more complex changes.
  — Charles Darwin, letter to Joseph Hooker, 1871

It's balmy April and the maple buds,
All swollen red and now prepared to burst,
Beckon me forth to make my first spring hike
Across the field and down the woodland path
To sit beside the overflowing stream
And watch its eddies and its swirls, its crests
When leaping over stones, its spume and spray,
Its rainbow mist that arcs the scene.
            I'll sit on a smooth outcropping of rock,
Entranced by light reflected from wet stones,
Light shimmering where water undulates,
Staring at the stark spectacle without
Insignias or tokens of my friends
Who've died within the year; I will return
To see curled water swoop within itself,
To dwell upon the wafted splash of light,
Determined only to observe.
                        Maybe
Old legs can't carry me so far this year;
Maybe I'll pack my lunch, but then turn back
Before I reach the stream if my hip won't
Obey my will's command; maybe for me
A final age of dwindling has begun,
And I'll return home with my blood subdued,

With disappointment shadowing my eyes
And only memory to serve as light,
My friends receding as I think of them,
Compelled to mull about our origins,
How water is our universal womb.

      My fear was accurate, although I tried
I couldn't make it to the chosen stream
And had to rest upon a rotting log before
I headed back, vowing to try again
In May or June, inspired, as Darwin was,
By "grandeur," nature's blind ability
To fabricate new complex forms, grandeur
Contending with profound dismay at nature's
Wastefulness — famine and violence,
An unrelenting process that began,
So awestruck Darwin would surmise, merely
By random chance in some warm little pond
According to a shift in chemistry.

      Well, I'm not ready to give in to gloom;
Perhaps next month with the incentive that
The fullness of spring blooming brings —
Bounty exceeding ravenous decay —
I'll give my legs and hip another try
To hike me to the stream. I've gotten fond
By now of all my groping body parts,
Although no longer can I count on them
As once I could, just to enjoy, to be
Aware I am aware, to be in touch —
With what exactly I don't know, to watch
The spume play on the surging water that
Still seems to welcome the indifferent light.

MIDDAY MOTHS

I am high stepping through the rough tall grass
Sparkling with daisies in the uncut field;
Meandering, I brush a path to pass
Through constellations of white moths concealed

Within their shaded midday resting place
Until chance footsteps stirred them into flight.
They populate my planetary space
As if to rearrange the fractured light,

As if berserk with awe, as I am now
Just watching them, quite unprepared as they
To know how to respond, just watching how
We're all propelled in our own startled way.

So what shall I, enraptured, make of this —
This whirling plenitude of randomness?

THIS INSTANT NOW

Right here, this instant now,
watching a nameless stream
whose waters leap over protruding rocks
and then flow twisting forth
as if a message were inherent there
which careful watching somehow
might disclose, I see stark noonday sun
in its reflected light,
effulgent in its vanishing,
this instant here, this here right now.

Reflections on the water's flow
repeat a theme in which what is
right here, this instant now,
might well shine forth
at any place or any time, and has —
one day lost in a multitude of days —
according to an unconsoling law
my watching faithfully obeys.

A sudden surge of wind reveals
the image of my face right here
upon one rock above the water
as I watch, the foam my beard,
a crevice in the rock my down-turned mouth —
a face that vanished right now
in the blazing instant it appeared.

Nearing an end, my own,
among an endless multitude of ends
stretched back as far as I can see,
I am no closer to where comfort was
or is or might forever be,
unless I find it merely in the sight
of water washing over gleaming stones,
reflections on which I reflect
and thus contain somehow,
even as liquid light eludes my witnessing
right here this instant now, and now again,
and now and now and now and now.

V. TWO EPILOGUES

THE WAR TO END ALL WARS

Despite the fact that I've lived long enough
to see the cold war end, the Berlin wall
come crashing down, nuclear weapons
used only as a threat to counteract
a counter threat, I fear next century,
incredibly, may be less kind to all
of us as the scenario of fate
unfolds according to what nature is —
I mean our own, what we must be at heart.
    I still cringe when a noise resounds, even
an urgent human voice addressing me
from right behind my stiffened back, as if,
with fast reflexes I've inherited
from our long evolutionary past,
I'm able to avoid oncoming bombs.
There's nothing new in how I still react.
    My mother as a Russian child survived
pogroms and blasts from raids; she'd hide
inside a closet when a thunderstorm
occurred. For her, the basic difference
between blind Nature's random violence
in storms or floods, and human viciousness,
deliberate and willed, had been obscured.
But she could find no consolation or
no innocence in the apparent fact
that people, like the elements, do what
they are designed to do — to fight, to hurt,
according to our native genius in

contriving instruments that make us more
what we have always been. And yet we ask:
Is it too late to choose to change ourselves —
perhaps if we get desperate enough?

      We have survived so far, though not without
tremendous suffering, starvation we
have caused, forced marches in the gouging sun;
only two atom bombs have been deployed
in half a century of brutal strife
about just whom the one god really loves
and whom he therefore wants us to destroy.
It's true we haven't quite gone all the way
in letting roiling hate obliterate
our sympathies — at least not yet, although
we're almost there, almost at the sharp edge
where genius to destroy, the genius that
defines us most as if technology,
inherent in our genes, waiting its time,
has brought us to the brink where now we are.

      Who is this "us"? Whose panting faces do
I conjure up when hot revenge bristles
my startled hair and burns inside my heart?
Because I mourn my own mortality,
do I indeed want everyone to die?
If I cannot survive myself, do I
desire to have all humankind go down
into the stinking mud along with me?
Can that face be my face or are there others
hidden in the hills, or else behind
pocked doors in alleyways of city slums
who wish extinction for my kind because —
because we don't believe what they believe.

So here I am again distracted by
the ideologies that seem the cause of why
we hate and why we kill, prepared to fight
the final futile war, despite the fact
that everywhere on this tormented earth
mothers protect their children, fathers risk
themselves to aid their wives, their friends, sometimes
for strangers pleading by the road — as you
cry to me now or maybe I to you.

MAKE-BELIEVE MY MUSE

I'm slumping at my desk, bereft,
my chin cupped in my hands,
my window open to a summer day
with red-tailed hawks that circle
in an updraft visible to them
as if they had eternity to hover there.
My muse, her wings transparent
as a darting dragonfly's,
a silver pitcher in her hand,
swoops with a whir into my room,
waters my plants, then flies to me
and whispers in harmonic tones,
"I before E except after C."
I like her sense of humor,
and I'm gratified, of course, to get
attention or advice of any kind,
but my mood darkens when she says,
"I'm sorry but I bring bad news —
the poem that you write next
may be your last; but don't lose cheer,
I bring good news as well:
thinking this poem may have to serve
as your own epitaph will help
increase your sense of urgency
in choosing what to write about."
Pleased with herself, unhurried, she
then waters all my plants again,

my jasmine, ivy, baby's tears,
and vanishes from whence she came,
aflame in her reflected light,
in the bronze dazzle of the morning sun.
　　Inspired by her, I ask myself what theme
might represent who I most truly am
in summing up my lifetime of depicting
trees and birds and animals and us
as here, astonishingly here,
yet equally perceiving everything
as vanishing into an emptiness
imagined as beyond imagining.
　　Themes of endurance and defeat
besiege my mind as inescapable:
the suffering of humankind,
betrayal, war — a mouth without a cry
expiring on a scorched-out battlefield —
how humankind collectively cannot
control blind hatred in deluded hearts.
　　The knowledge of each other
that a couple shares in silence
after years of tending children
in their bottomless dependency
also seems immemorial to me
and might possess the ache to shape
into a soothing song of sweet lament.
　　Maybe friendship might be my most
defined, distinguishable choice —
praising those who maintain their loyalty
when one's position and one's power are lost,

one's titles, gone, and all one has to offer
is one's caring and one's company.
        Each theme seems worthy of a final poem,
so how can I choose only one?
I need another lifetime to decide,
a lifetime like the first — the same wedged geese
still flying through — that honors what
it almost perfectly repeats, although
such wishing constitutes another theme.
        Maybe my choosing something small,
believable, so the mere fact of it
seems casual and insignificant,
might happily suffice and be
the proper subject for my final poem.
Maybe a luminescent dragonfly
who rests by chance a moment on a leaf
of that familiar twisted apple tree
beyond my window's opening
to which wild turkeys, wary deer,
come in late fall to browse and eat
fermented apples on the wobbly ground
says everything I need to say
about my passing and my being here.
        And yet perhaps I'd best content myself
just savoring the resonance of words,
their undulating sounds like water
flowing over stones, like notes
that can be given order, given form —
a rainbow melody that means
what each rapt listener feels that it means:

some pitched high with excitement like
a word containing the bright letter I,
or one made melancholy with a wailing E,
a vowel echoing itself, as in eternity,
or one that crisply puts forth C,
as does companionship,
composed in its exquisite brevity.